BOUNDARIES

Saving Yourself
Until Marriage

Dr. Paula C. Perez

DrP & Me, LLC

TABLE OF CONTENTS

FOREWORD

My phone rings and it is Dr. Paula Perez returning my very vague email. As we began to talk, I could tell in her voice she had solid plans and was ready for action. She had an attitude that invoked enthusiasm and excitement. As we were talking, I became even more excited because I could feel her passion for the work and vision that God had given her. It was clear to me that she was dedicated and determined to reach and inform as many individuals as possible with a book of resources that could assist them in the journey to live a life of celibacy.

"Dr. Perez's book *Boundaries* uses an acronym to provide strategies and support for remaining celibate until marriage." There are ten words that are coupled with Scripture to give you strategies and support to assist you on your journey of celibacy until you get married. She talks candidly about her own struggles and successes, and she reminds us that we all have a journey and there is growth and success. This book of resources is only as good as the reader or user. There must be a time of dedication and reflection in order that you can take control of your life and the power that God has given you within. She includes those that were previously sexually active and acknowledges "second virginity" Dr. Perez makes it noticeably clear as she informs all that it includes all forms of sex.

Boundaries is well put together giving why you need boundaries plus what they should mean to you. It also addresses what if you have been sexually active. It tells one how to get ready. It gives you the format of the book and how to effectively use it. The book is written so that males or females or both can learn from it. It can be used individually by yourself, in a group, or by you and someone else. There is also a poem in the book that addresses boundaries. She covers a lot of ground including solo sex (masturbation) and pornography and the married.

Professionally qualified and equipped with an extended education and experience in living a life of celibacy, Dr. Perez's life tells the story and her life is the witness. Her greatest qualifying factors are her trust and faith in the God that we serve who has given her the vision and the tools to accomplish such a task. She is also a SYMBIS (Saving Your Marriage Before It Starts) counselor and has been around children and young people for most of her life. She has been both a teacher and principal and has worn many other hats. She is currently a pastor's wife and a counselor.

Dr. Perez has done the Word as stated in Habakkuk:

> And the LORD answered me: "Write the vision; make it plain on tablets, so he may run who reads it. For still the vision awaits its appointed time; it hastens to the end—it will not lie. If it seems slow, wait for it; it will surely come; it will not delay." (Habakkuk 2:2–3 ESV)

The book has much-needed information and it also comes with references for follow-up and further support for your journey of celibacy. *Boundaries* is a dedicated read for those who are serious about the journey to celibacy.

Evangelist Mary Lewis-Freeman

BEFORE YOU BEGIN

If you picked up this book, you or someone you care about is attempting to date in a God-honoring way. You desire to follow the principles ascribed in the Bible about sex before marriage. This book will help you commit to abstinence and achieve your goal of remaining celibate until marriage. In doing so, you will bring a unique bond to your marriage offering you incomparable personal growth opportunities that can be gleaned only through your experience of abstinence until marriage.

I boldly make this assertion because it worked for me. I lived a full life as a single woman, impacting countless lives. On my thirty-three–year celibacy journey, the Lord enabled me to experience success. And when I finally married, I was able to present my body to my spouse knowing he would receive the gift of my virginity.

Yes, you read that correctly. It was a thirty-three–year commitment to celibacy. When I was sixteen, I vowed before my parents and God not to have sex of any kind until I was married. What I did not know is that it would take over three decades for this promise to be fulfilled. I wrote about it in my memoir, *49-Year-Old Virgin: Delayed Not Denied.*

For more information on how I can help you with my *Saving Yourself for Marriag*e and my *YANA (You Are Not Alone)* classes or to get my fees for retreats, conferences, and relationship events, email info@drpaulacperez.com.

INTRODUCTION

◆─◇─◦── ◉ ──◦─◇─◆

As you enter into relationships, you must consider your rules for engagement. In other words, you must decide what is okay and what crosses the line in your interaction with your partner. You must wrestle with what treatment you are willing to give and what you expect to get. For example, because I knew my worth in Christ, when a man I was dating raised his hand to strike me, I did not hesitate to close the door to that relationship. It ended right there at that moment. I knew

I was fearfully and wonderfully made, and I was not going to allow anyone to beat on my "temple." Our actions teach people how to treat us. Do you love yourself enough to demand the respect you deserve?

All healthy, loving relationships have boundaries that protect you emotionally, physically, and spiritually. As a person committed to remaining celibate until you are married, understanding the purpose of these boundaries can also help you openly discuss your convictions about all forms of sex and enable you to remain celibate.

THE PURPOSE OF BOUNDARIES

Understanding the purpose of boundaries will help you embrace the tenets in this text, including:

- Maintaining personal space and privacy:
  Boundaries help to define a person's physical, emotional, and psychological space and ensure that it is respected by others.

- Facilitating healthy relationships:
  Boundaries help people communicate their needs, wants, and expectations in relationships and facilitate mutual respect and understanding.

- Promoting personal responsibility:
  Boundaries help individuals take responsibility for their actions, thoughts, and emotions and avoid blaming others.

- Protecting emotional and physical well-being: Boundaries help people protect themselves from emotional, spiritual, psychological, and physical harm.

- Establishing clear and effective communication: Boundaries help to clearly communicate what is acceptable and unacceptable behavior.

Like the snail that protects its inner core by creating a barrier around its body, so it is with the boundaries drawn in God's Word. As you work through this book, you will read several Bible verses that speak to these boundaries. They are there for our protection. Our dating boundaries can also help protect our internal parts: our mind, body, and spirit.

WHAT ARE THE BOUNDARIES?

In this book, BOUNDARIES is an acronym used to show you how to remain celibate until marriage.

B –	**Believe**
O –	**Obey** His Word
U –	**Understand** His Principles
N –	**Normalize** No Wed, No Bed
D –	**Develop** Self-Control
A –	**Ask** Accountability Partners
R –	**Renew** Your Mind
I –	**Improve** Your Impact
E –	**Embrace** Truth
S –	**Show** Self-Love

This book explores strategies to help you keep your vow of abstinence from sexual impurity. To be clear, I am talking about all forms of sex.

I'm surprised how many, young and old, justify having anal or oral sex outside of marriage. Contrary to what one president said, if *sex* is in the phrase, *it is SEX!* So, when I talk about abstinence, I mean refraining from all forms: vaginal, anal, and oral sex. Engaging in these types of relationships with your partner before marriage will have an impact not only on your relationship with your partner but also on your relationship with God. Refer to the Related Topics section for more information on sexual behaviors that will compromise you and make it difficult to remain celibate.

WHAT IF IT IS ALREADY TOO LATE?

This book is too late for me. I am no longer a virgin. Where was this book when I was a teenager?

Regardless of your situation, whether you have lost your virginity through choice or force, it is never too late to change course. Perhaps you are a widow or divorced. Taking a vow of celibacy still makes sense in this season of your life. You can still experience the benefits of choosing not to have sex until you marry. The fact that you've read this far says you are interested in surrounding your single life with boundaries.

I am not sure who coined the phrase *second virginity*. However, that is a great way to view the decision to abstain from sex until marriage. No, you cannot return your body to that state it was in before you had intercourse. However, you can reset your emotional and spiritual state. By choosing this path you can:

- Have emotional clarity: Celibacy can allow you to focus on your emotional needs and desires without the added complexity of sexual relationships. This can help you gain clarity about your own values, goals, and priorities as well as what you want in a future partner.

- Have a stronger bond with your partner: If you choose to remain celibate until marriage, you can build a strong emotional and intellectual bond with your partner before adding physical intimacy to the mix. This can create a deeper connection and sense of trust between you, which can enhance your relationship over time.

- Avoid STIs: By abstaining from sexual activity until marriage, you reduce your risk of contracting sexually transmitted infections (STIs), which can have serious long-term health consequences.

- Avoid unintended pregnancy: Celibacy also eliminates the risk of unintended pregnancy, which can have major implications for your life plans and goals.

- Avoid potential emotional pain: Sex can be emotionally complicated, and engaging in it before you're ready or with someone who isn't a good match for you can lead to heartache and pain. By waiting until marriage, you reduce the risk of experiencing these negative consequences.

- Avoid negative soul ties: Sex is not just a physical act. It also involves your soul. Connecting with the wrong person will leave an unwelcomed residue on your life. Remember, there is no such thing as *casual sex*.

- Attain personal growth: Celibacy can be a way to challenge yourself and grow personally. It can help you develop self-control and discipline, which can be valuable skills in many areas of life including your future marriage.

- Develop a closer relationship with Christ: Obeying God's principle for dating and avoiding sex outside of marriage will result in a deeper relationship with the Lord. You can approach your heavenly Father without guilt or shame.

So, regardless of your past, determine to change your future. Remember Satan's job is to entangle you in his snare so he can destroy you and your destiny.

If you have fallen into the devil's trap, remember God's grace is sufficient. Our heavenly Father is waiting with his arms open wide to embrace you in his love. The great thing is God forgives and forgets. So forgive yourself and get back into the "celibacy pool." Then rely on the Lord's power to see you through.

GET READY

Now that I've laid the groundwork, make sure you write down your "aha" moments. There is something about the physical act of writing. It will help you remember the material.

Now, it's time to get to work on the boundaries. In addition to your Bible, grab a journal or notebook for your journey. The physical act of writing helps to solidify the learning. So write down your reflections and "aha" moments. Now, if you have your books in hand, let's begin.

WHAT'S YOUR WHY?

Simon Sinek, in his book entitled *Start with Why: How Great Leaders Inspire Everyone to Take Action*, talks about the significance of understanding the reasoning behind your decisions. In other words, knowing your "why" is crucial to your success in any venture. So, as you think about your decision to remain celibate, begin by thinking about your why. What is the reasoning behind your decision to remain abstinent? If you are committed to your why, it will help you stick to your vow of celibacy.

Perhaps you have given your life to Christ, and you have heard it said that you should not sleep with your partner before marriage. Maybe you have done something different all your life, but now you are ready for a change. You think, *I might as well try this.* Whatever your reason, be sure you can articulate your why.

Now it's time to discuss the building blocks which serve as boundaries in our lives. So, grab your notebook and a Bible then begin our journey together.

FORMAT OF THIS BOOK

Each chapter discusses a letter in the acronym B.O.U.N.D.A.R.I.E.S. Although the chapters are sequenced to spell out the word, you may read them in any order.

This book contains ten tips and each lesson has five components. An easy way to remember them is the word DRIVE, which stands for:

- **D** – **Describe** one of the boundary blocks
- **R** – **Read** the Bible verses
- **I** – **Identify** areas in your life in need of growth
- **V** – **Visualize/Verbalize** what you need to do
- **E** – **Embark** on your journey. Put your action steps in motion.

HOW TO USE THIS BOOK

This book is designed for use with individuals and groups. Whether you are working alone or with some friends, I encourage you to have a Bible, pen, and notebook.

For Individuals:

Plan on spending 30–45 minutes on each lesson. Eliminate distractions so you can focus while you are studying. Read the boundary area description and the associated Bible verses. As you read the Scriptures, highlight key words and jot down notes.

Then work through the remaining three sections: Identify, Visualize/Verbalize, and Embark.

Remember, handwriting your thoughts—"inking your thinking"—rather than typing your notes will help you process the material.

For Groups:

Here are some suggestions for using this material in groups. Plan to spend 60–90 minutes in your group time. There are two options for proceeding.

- As a group, work through the material. Begin by reading the description of the boundary area. Then work through the remaining four sections: Read, Identify, Visualize/Verbalize, and Embark on your celibacy journey.

- Group members work through the lessons before the group session. Once in the group, use the time to ask questions and get clarification on the principles. Use the group to hold one another accountable for the work during this study. Set aside 60–75 minutes to follow the outline:

  1. Opening Prayer
  2. Check-In. Members report on individual goals

3. Discuss the boundary area

4. Q/A regarding the topic

5. Next Steps. Members fill in the blank, "Next week I will _____."

6. Closing Prayer

Now that you've decided which path to take, reflect on the poem on the next page.

BOUNDARIES

an original poem by P. Perez and AI

Boundaries in relationships, a guide to remain celibate,

A journey through love, where one should never hesitate

To set the limits, to protect your heart,

A path of self-discovery, perhaps a fresh start,

A time to reflect, to understand what's true,

A time to find peace, in all that you do,

To recognize the limits, to know what you need,

And to stay within the lines, where true love can succeed.

It's not always easy, to stay on this course,

With temptations and desires that can cause a divorce

From the principles, the values that you hold so dear,

But with strong boundaries, your love will remain sincere.

So hold on tight to the path you have chosen,

And never let go of the love that's not broken.

For with strong boundaries, your heart will remain pure,

And your love will flourish, forever to endure.

So trust in yourself, trust in God's love,

And never compromise the blessings from above,

For with strong boundaries, your love will shine bright,

A beacon of hope, in a world of darkness and night.

Let's Go !

BOUNDARIES

1. BELIEVE

DESCRIBE:

You must believe that you can remain celibate until marriage. This task is easier if you couple that with a belief in Jesus. That is the foundation of all things. The Bible says in Philippians 2:5, "In your relationships with one another, have the same mindset as Christ Jesus . . ." How do we know Jesus's mindset? We must know Him!

We cultivate our relationship with the Lord by prioritizing it. Determine to make him first in your life. Exodus 20 and Deuteronomy 5 tell us that God is a jealous God and does not want us to have anything before him, including the pursuit of a mate. Many people have fallen on the "altar of sex" outside of marriage by elevating sex to the position of God. Perhaps that is why people struggle in the area of sex.

READ:

Exodus 20:3–5; Deuteronomy 5:7–10: Matthew 6:33; Psalm 37:4; Philippians 4:13

IDENTIFY:

There was a time I was obsessed with being in a relationship and getting married. I made the pursuit of finding my mate, my god. I thought more of that type of relationship than I did of my relationship with the Lord. What have you elevated in your life to the position of God? In what ways do you need to prioritize God in your life?

VISUALIZE/VERBALIZE:

List the top two things hindering you from putting God first. Visualize what putting God first in your life looks like. Jot it down. Then voice a prayer to the Lord regarding your journey and ask him for direction.

EMBARK:

Write down your next steps. What are you going to do differently?

2. OBEY GOD'S WORD

DESCRIBE:

It is not enough to read the Bible. We must do what it says. God's word, like a guardrail, is there for protection. However, it is comforting to know, if you fall or "break through the guardrail," you can get back up and recommit to doing things God's way. God forgives and forgets. His grace gives us chance after chance to get this right. When we ask God for his forgiveness and help not to fall into sexual temptation, he empowers us to keep our commitment in this area. So, obey God's truths and live your life in a way that pleases the Lord.

READ:

Philippians 4:19; Deuteronomy 11:1; 2 Corinthians 10:5; Revelation 14:12; John 14:15; James 1:22

IDENTIFY:

After reading the verses, which verses have you been ignoring or finding obsolete?

VISUALIZE/VERBALIZE:

There are times when we know the truth, but still ignore it. We have head knowledge about a subject, but we have not embraced it and applied it to our lives. How will your life change if you stop just reading (or listening to) the Word of God, and start *doing* what it says by putting it into practice and applying it to your life?

EMBARK:

This week what are you going to do differently? What steps are you going to take to put God's Word into action?

3. UNDERSTAND GOD'S PRINCIPLES

⊷◇─◇── ◉ ──◇─◇⊶

DESCRIBE:

If we are to save ourselves until marriage, we must understand God's principles, the third step in putting BOUNDARIES in place. A principle is a fundamental truth that is foundational to our faith in Christ. The Bible does not specifically cite every possible dating scenario. You will not find the word *dating* in the Bible. However, the principles are embedded in God's Word. Take time to understand the underlying truths that should govern your behavior in relationships. Remember, "in all thy getting, get understanding" (Proverbs 4:7). Living by God's principles will help rid you of guilt and shame and help set you up for a marriage based on trust, discipline, and mutual respect making your marriage a rich and fulfilling relationship.

What is the purpose of dating and how does it differ from courtship? Quah and Kumagai define dating "as the activities intended to establish and pursue a romantic relationship and, consequently, dating occurs only in social contexts that permit romantic love. In contrast to the simple definition of dating, let us understand by courtship all the activities intended to establish and formalize the relationship between two persons, for the purpose of matrimony."[1]

---

[1] Quah, S.R., ed. (2015) "Dating and Courtship". Routledge Handbook of Families in Asia. London: Routledge, p 111.

Simply put, dating is a social activity and an end in itself, while courtship is for the explicit purpose of marriage. Is it possible that dating prepares us for divorce while courtship prepares us for matrimony? So I ask you again, what is your end goal?

READ:

Proverbs 3:5-6; James 1:5; Proverbs 2:1–6; Hebrews 13:4; 2 Corinthians 6:14–15; 1 Corinthians 7:39

IDENTIFY:

Study the Bible verses. Based on the verses, what principles can you identify for relationships? What other Bible verses give you insight into godly principles for relationships or sex?

VISUALIZE/VERBALIZE:

What is your end goal for a romantic relationship? How do God's principles instruct your behavior in relationships? In other words, what should you continue to do, and what should you stop doing to align your relationship with God's principles?

EMBARK:

As you go through this week, seek God and ask him to open up your understanding. Write your prayer here:

4. NORMALIZE NO WED, NO BED

DESCRIBE:

This step is the easiest to say, but depending on your circumstances, it may be the hardest to keep. The Bible is very clear on this point. Paul tells us, "Marriage is to be held in honor among all [that is, regarded as something of great value], and the marriage bed undefiled [by immorality or by any sexual sin]; for God will judge the sexually immoral and adulterous" (Hebrews 13:4 AMP, brackets in original).

It is indeed difficult to meet God's standard. But I'm a living witness that it *is* possible. If God requires something of us, he gives us the necessary tools to accomplish it. This is the role of the Holy Spirit. He empowers us to say no. The Spirit gives us the self-control needed to turn down temptation. He always provides a way to escape!

The way of escape provided by the Holy Spirit requires something of us as well. We need to stop providing the opportunity for sexual temptation. The temptation is not wrong. Even Jesus was tempted. However, we must be prepared to respond when that temptation comes. For instance, set boundaries around how late you will stay out. Think about it; what good can come of hanging out at a boyfriend's house after 9 or 10 p.m.? Don't park on "Lovers' Lane." Let your accountability partners know where you are going.

What if you have already had sex? That's what I love about the Lord—his grace will cover us. Start afresh today. Ask the Lord to forgive you; then forgive yourself! Decide once and for all that you will remain celibate until you get married.

READ:

1 Corinthians 7:2; Hebrews 13:4; 1 Thessalonians 4:3–5; Galatians 5:19; Ephesians 5:3

IDENTIFY:

What in your past has contributed to your sexual decisions? How do the verses you read inform your decision about sex outside of marriage? How does having oral sex or anal sex outside of marriage impact your relationships? Think about the settings and environments that put you in the mood for having sex. Is it a movie or television show? Perhaps it is being at your partner's house after dark. Be aware of the time of the month when you become horny!

VISUALIZE/VERBALIZE:

The Bible says you are the temple of the Holy Spirit. Visualize yourself as a church. Then imagine having sex in the pews as Holy Spirit looks upon you. Would you still have intercourse?

EMBARK:

Write down at least three safeguards you will put in place to avoid being tempted to have sex outside of marriage.

5. DEVELOP SELF-CONTROL

DESCRIBE:

Many people's concept of love is *What can I get out of it?* They want to have their needs met, and they want it now. They feel that if you love them, you will buy them things. If you love them, you will do whatever they say. If you love them, you will sleep with them. You will fulfill their sexual cravings even though you are not married. They justify having oral or even anal sex with their unmarried partner. Might this be a selfish kind of love?

In our hearts, we know true love desires to give. True love enables you to put your partner's well-being ahead of your selfish desires. As the apostle Paul says, God has given us the power to control ourselves. Paul tells us in 2 Timothy 1:7, that "the Spirit God gave us does not make us timid, but gives us power, love, and self-discipline." True love involves self-control. "For the grace of God has appeared that offers salvation to all people. It teaches us to say 'No' to ungodliness and worldly passions and to live self-controlled, upright, and godly lives in this present age" (Titus 2:11–12). If you are to remain celibate until marriage, you must develop self-control. "Resist the Devil and he will flee from you" (James 4:4–8).

READ:

Proverbs 25:28; 1 Corinthians 9:27; Titus 2:11-12; Galatians 5:22-23; 2 Peter 1:5-6

IDENTIFY:

In what area of your dating life do you need to regain control?

VISUALIZE/VERBALIZE:

Visualize how you will act and express yourself in the dating world while keeping God's promise.

EMBARK:

Write down the godly characteristics you strive to emulate and so look forward to discovering in your mate.

6. ASK ACCOUNTABILITY PARTNERS

DESCRIBE:

Throughout my life, I was very fortunate to be surrounded by wise counsel. It is really important to have people that you can rely on for sound advice, especially in the area of your relationships.

I encourage you to find one or two accountability partners you can entrust with information about your dating life. Things are always easier when you partner with a trusted friend. Choose someone who is aligned with the biblical principles for dating. Do not just find someone who will say what you want them to say. As you select this person, you need to feel comfortable with them asking you specific questions about your sex life. Choose people who will hold you accountable to your celibacy journey. Permit them to ask you tough questions about the physical and emotional nature of your relationship. Remember, they are there to help you stay within the boundaries.

> Two are better than one, because they have a good return for their labor: If either of them falls down, one can help the other up. But pity anyone who falls and has no one to help them up. (Ecclesiastes 4:9–10 NIV)

READ:

Proverbs 19:20; Proverbs 15:22; Proverbs 12:15

IDENTIFY:

Who might you include on your accountability team? Be sure they are people who understand your goal and can help hold you accountable.

VISUALIZE/VERBALIZE:

Visualize how you will act and express yourself in the dating world while keeping God's promise. Ask your accountability partner to keep you in check in those areas.

EMBARK:

Develop a list of questions you want your accountability partner to ask you regularly.

7. RENEW YOUR MIND

DESCRIBE:

You want to keep your vow to remain celibate, but you are still struggling. Why? Perhaps you are challenged by the expectations of your peers. After all, isn't everyone doing it? The answer is *no*! Change your thoughts around this area. You will not be the only one who is not having sex. See yourself being successful in this area. You must remember that every action starts with a thought! So change your thinking. I know, you are

DR. PAULA C. PEREZ

probably saying, "Easier said than done." Yes, it may be challenging, but it is possible.

Dr. Caroline Leaf is a world-renowned specialist in the area of cognitive neuroscience. She is a Christian who specializes in the area of cognitive and metacognitive neuropsychology. What I love about her work is she shows how the science works behind Scriptures like "Do not conform to the pattern of this world, but be transformed by the renewing of your mind. Then you will be able to test and approve what God's will is—his good, pleasing and perfect will" (Romans 12:2 KJV).

She has written several books on the topic. Two of my favorites are Switch on Your Brain: The Key to Peak Happiness, Thinking, and Health and Cleaning Up Your Mental Mess: 5 Simple, Scientifically Proven Steps to Reduce Anxiety, Stress, and Toxic Thinking.

Dr. Leaf also has several videos in which she talks about these topics on YouTube. Check them out.

I also recommend you use the filter of Philippians 4:8–9 to determine whether something is beneficial or detrimental to your goal of remaining celibate. The verse says, "Finally, brothers and sisters, whatever is true, whatever is noble, whatever is right, whatever is pure, whatever is lovely, whatever is admirable—if anything is excellent or praiseworthy—think about such things. Whatever you have learned or received or heard from me, or seen in me—put it into practice. And the God of peace will be with you."

READ:

Romans 12:1-2; 2 Corinthians 5:17; 2 Corinthians 3:18 Psalm 51:10; 2 Corinthians 10:3–5; Ephesians 4:22–24

IDENTIFY:

In educational realms, we use the term "stinking thinking" with our students, which refers to those negative thoughts that result in self-sabotage. In what area of your thought life about relationships do you have unhealthy thoughts? In what way has the media or the culture corrupted your thinking or values?

VISUALIZE/VERBALIZE:

Adjust your television and online viewing to shows and media that do not corrupt your values.

EMBARK:

Discontinue cable and streaming services that pollute your mind. (Save your money!) Investigate Dr. Leaf's strategies; then put them in place.

8. IMPROVE YOUR IMPACT

—○—○— ◉ —○—○—

DESCRIBE:

W e've all been placed here for a purpose. Have you discovered yours? I guarantee you part of the reason you exist is to invest in the lives of others. There is something to be said about increasing your impact on the world. So while you are still single and blessed to have the time to pursue these opportunities, think of ways you can share your gifts of compassion, loyalty, and friendship.

Consider furthering your education. That's what I did. I earned my doctorate before I got married. This enabled me to have a larger platform, thus increasing my impact on others.

Are there other volunteer opportunities that you can take advantage of in this season of your life? For instance, I started a not-for-profit called King's Kids. This allowed me to impact the lives of hundreds of children. In addition to helping them with their schoolwork, we also helped them develop their gifts and talents.

In this season while you are still single, you must also learn how to receive. This is especially true if you want to be married. Learning to receive can be challenging for some people. They may feel uncomfortable accepting help or gifts from others, or they may feel like they don't deserve it. But receiving is just as important as giving, and learning how to do it graciously is important.

Some women give off a vibe that they do not need a man because they are unwilling to receive their chivalrous acts like opening the door or the man's offer to carry their packages. You will be amazed at the impact of simply saying thank you and acknowledging the generosity of others. This strengthens your relationships and creates a deeper sense of connection. So, don't be afraid to accept help. Whether it is help with moving, cooking dinner, or just listening to you vent, accepting help can make a big difference in your life and theirs.

READ:

Matthew 5:16; 1 Peter 4:10; 1 Corinthians 15:58; 1 Corinthians 10:31; Colossians 3:17; Galatians 6:9

IDENTIFY:

What are your strengths? What are you passionate about? In what areas do you need to show more gratitude?

VISUALIZE/VERBALIZE:

Think about where your passion and your purpose collide. In other words, consider the intersection of your strengths and passion. What can you start doing in that area? Visualize yourself doing what you are passionate about and verbalize that thing to a loved one for their support.

EMBARK:

Develop a life that is filled with gratitude. Take an inventory or spiritual assessment to learn more about your strengths and weaknesses. There are many free ones available on the internet. Scan the QR code or click on the links to these resources:

https://giftstest.com/

https://spiritualgiftstest.com/

https://mintools.com/spiritual-gifts-test.htm

https://www.lifethrive.com/spiritual-gifts-assessment/

9. EMBRACE TRUTH

DESCRIBE:

Your dating life is an opportunity to collect data. As you see things, honestly examine them. Listen to the alarms that go off in your head, then embrace the truth. Recognize that your dating life not only reveals things about your partner, but your relationship will also reveal facts about you!

Perhaps you are not currently dating. If the right person came along, are you ready to be in a relationship? What is your financial status? Do you know how to take care of a home? Will you be an asset or a liability to your potential mate? Consider if you are capable of being someone's purpose partner. This necessitates you knowing your purpose! Do not shy away from the truth but hold on to it and let it set you free.

READ:

John 8:32; John 16:13; Psalm 119:160; Colossians 3:9; Ephesians 4:15; 2 Timothy 2:15; John 3:21

IDENTIFY:

What are the red flags in your life? What do you need to change? What should you keep? What or who might you need to shed?

VISUALIZE/VERBALIZE:

What is the truth about you? What is the truth about your relationship, if you are in one?

EMBARK:

Ask your close family and friends to reveal potential blind spots in your life. If you are still struggling with past hurts or trauma, seek professional help. Find a list of potential counselors or speak to your spiritual leader

10. SHOW SELF-LOVE

DESCRIBE:

Self-love is the outward expression and appreciation for your individual physical, emotional, and spiritual well-being. You need to learn to prioritize these areas in your life over others, recognizing that if you are empty, you will not be able to pour into another person's life.

Before you can love anyone else, you must learn to love yourself. Heal the places that are hurt before embarking upon a relationship.

"Jesus replied: 'Love the Lord your God with all your heart and with all your soul and with all your mind.' This is the first and greatest commandment. And the second is like it: 'Love your neighbor as yourself.' All the Law and the Prophets hang on these two commandments." (Matthew 22:37–40)

"Many, O LORD my God, are the wonders You have done, and the plans You have for us—none can compare to You—if I proclaim and declare them, they are more than I can count" (Psalm 40:5).

READ:

Mark 12:30-31; Psalm 139:13-14; Matthew 10:30-31; Ephesians 5:29; 1 Timothy 4:14; Matthew 6:25

IDENTIFY:

Who are you? What do you love about yourself? How do you pamper yourself? When was the last time you took yourself on a date?

VISUALIZE/VERBALIZE:

What makes you feel good about yourself? What do you enjoy doing by yourself? What activities do you enjoy doing with a friend?

EMBARK:

Write down ten affirmations about yourself. Pick a day this week and love on yourself for at least an hour.

RELATED TOPICS

SOLO SEX

This book would not be complete without a discussion of areas that may impact people as they navigate being celibate until marriage. The topics in this section include a discussion of having sex by yourself as well as some comments on singles that have trouble switching their brains on and embracing their sexual freedom once they are married.

MASTURBATION

Masturbation is the stimulation of one's own genitals (clitoris or penis) for personal pleasure. People masturbate with their hands or an object such as a sex toy. It is usually done alone. I refer to it as "self-sex."

The Bible does not specifically mention the topic of masturbation. However, there are principles within Scriptures that we should use as a guide.

> Flee from sexual immorality. All other sins a person commits are outside the body, but whoever sins sexually, sins against their own body. Do you not know that your bodies are temples of the Holy Spirit, who is in you, whom you have received from God? You are not your own; you were bought at a price. Therefore honor God with your bodies. (1 Corinthians 6:18-20 NIV)

For many, masturbation is a completely normal and healthy way to enjoy and explore their body. It is used as a stress reliever and a means of improving their mood. I've heard it said that it can help one sleep better.

Hmm, so what are the possible repercussions? There are many. And as person attempting to live your single years in a God-honoring way, masturbation is not the way.

> But among you there must not be even a hint of sexual immorality, or of any kind of impurity, or of greed, because these are improper for God's holy people. Nor should there be obscenity, foolish talk or coarse joking, which are out of place, but rather thanksgiving. For of this you can be sure: No immoral, impure or greedy person—such a person is an idolater—has any inheritance in the kingdom of Christ and of God. (Ephesians 5:3-5 NIV)

"Why not?" you ask. Masturbation can be habit-forming. Instead of controlling your flesh, your body begins to control you. As with any addictive behavior, this often leads to other sinful behaviors. You will need to do it more and more to get the same affect.

Because masturbation is an act done usually in private, it may also heighten your sense of loneliness. This may lead to feelings of depression and maybe even anxiety.

Masturbating hampers your future ability to be intimate with your mate. Self-gratification in this way sets up a selfish expectation of what sex should look like in your marriage relationship. Often, the partner that masturbates does not enter the sexual relationship focused on giving, but only on how to satisfy their own sexual desire. This will leave their partner unfulfilled and often feeling used.

Every sin starts with a thought. The more you feed your mind with messages that violate God's principles the more prone you will be to try them. So be careful what you watch. Ask the Lord to guard your heart and transform your mind. But it is not enough to just pray. You have a role to play in this process. You must exercise self-control.

Once the sexual desire is stirred up, especially outside of marriage, it can be difficult, but not impossible, to put it back into the proverbial bottle and keep it contained until marriage. Remember, you can do all things through Christ who gives you the strength you need (Philippians 4:13).

As apostle Paul said, we all need to learn to discipline our body and keep it under control (1 Corinthians 9:27). So filter what you take into your senses through the lens of Philippians 4.

> Finally, brothers and sisters, whatever is true, whatever is noble, whatever is right, whatever is pure, whatever is lovely, whatever is admirable—if anything is excellent or praiseworthy—think about such things. Whatever you

have learned or received or heard from me, or seen in me—put it into practice. And the God of peace will be with you. (Philippians 4:8–9 NIV)

Remember, it is easier to contain the sexual energy than try to bottle it back up after it is unleashed. Once your senses are awakened, it may be difficult, but not impossible, to contain. You will need to seek the power that comes only from the Holy Spirit to give you the strength to avoid yielding to temptation. You will need to rely on all the "fruit of the Spirit," including patience and self-control.

Pray and ask the Lord to give you self-control in this area. If you belong to Him, you will be able to distinguish His voice from all the others out there. Jesus is willing and able to lead you in this area. Let him!

I'm a witness to the Lord's keeping power. He kept me from getting into all types of sexual sins, including pornography.

PORNOGRAPHY

In the book of Matthew, Jesus takes the seventh commandment to a new level. He tells the people that they have heard that it's wrong to commit adultery (sex with someone that is not your spouse); this includes fornication (having sex outside of marriage). Jesus took it even further by indicating if you even look at another person with the desire to have sex with them, you are committing adultery in your heart (Matthew 5:27–28). From this, one may imply that any pornography is a sin.

There are millions of sites designed to lure your eyes and impact your thought processes so you crave its content. Because of the ubiquitous nature of digital pornography, it is more accessible than ever before. One just needs to reach for their phone. Whether intended or not, porn has a way of ending up on any device connected to the internet. Porn is big business. This is dangerous because pornography can lead to addiction, desensitization, and a distorted view of sex and relationships.

Statistics reveal that the increase in the amount and reach of pornography cannot be ignored. But it is not just a problem affecting men. Women, teenagers, and children are also being caught in the web of pornography at alarming rates.

Not only has pornography invaded churches, but in many cases, the statistics show that Christians—and even pastors—engage in viewing porn at almost the same rates as the secular population[2].

Pornography is an enterprise that the Barna group studied in 2016.[3] They sought to answer two questions: To what extent has pornography permeated Christian families, the church, and our society at large? And what

---

[2] Wiles, Jeremy. (May 5, 2022). https://conquerseries.com/15-mind-blowing-statistics-about-pornography-and-the-church (Accessed April 13, 2023)

[3] The statistics in the following paragraphs are taken from Josh McDowell. *The Porn Phenomenon: The Impact of Pornography in the Digital Age* (Barna Group, 2016).

has been the impact of this porn accessibility? According to 94 percent of youth pastors and 93 percent of pastors questioned, porn is a much bigger or somewhat bigger issue in the church than it was in the past.

In 2016, 41 percent of practicing Christian males aged 13–24 used porn at least once per month. However, women struggle in this area too. The study reported that 13 percent of Christian females aged 13–24 also watched porn at the same frequency.

This exposure to pornography is dangerous. While it may seem harmless or even enjoyable, pornography can negatively impact your mental, emotional, and spiritual health.

If you struggle in this area, here are a few resources that may help you. Scan the QR code or click on the links:

https://sherecovery.com/

www.TheJourneyCourse.com

https://theFreedomFight.org

Xxxchurch.com

I'M MARRIED.
NOW WHAT?

There are some people who, after programming their bodies not to have sex for so long, have trouble turning their sex drive back on once they get married. They feel guilty for allowing their body to feel all the sensations and emotions that may come with having sex. I believe this stems from the feeling that sex is dirty or nasty.

Read the Song of Solomon in the Old Testament of the Bible. You will see the beautiful expression of love that the couple shared. Hopefully, this will remind you that you have the right to enjoy your spouse!

If you are still struggling in this area, or if intercourse is painful, seek out help. It may be as simple as adding lubrication. (Coconut oil is perfect and a natural remedy for dryness.)

You may also need help reprogramming your thoughts. Some church teaching, in an effort to keep us from having sex outside of marriage, has made us feel like sex is nasty or dirty rather than teaching us that sex is beautiful and something that God invented, but for the exclusive use in a marriage relationship.

Perhaps you have experienced sexual trauma in your past. Someone molested or raped you. Seek a counselor or therapist to deal with it. Remember, Satan is in the secrets. The devil loves to get into your thoughts and make you feel like everything is your fault. By uncovering and confronting your secrets, you regain your power. No one can hold the event over your head as a threat. A trained expert can help you move the "dirt" and find the proverbial "roots" so you can pull them out.

Finally, remember: God invented sex, and everything that God made is good. Take the time to understand your anatomy and your partner's. Sometimes you have not because you ask not. So communicate about what you like and don't like sexually.

CONCLUSION

You did it! You completed the steps. So if you were already on this path, by all means, continue! If you are just now grasping the need to remain celibate until marriage, congratulations. I believe you have made the right choice.

Please know I am here to help you along your journey. As a Saving Your Marriage Before It Starts (SYMBIS) counselor, I can help you unearth issues that need to be addressed for you to have a healthy relationship.

Feel free to reach out to me at MeetDrPaula.com or on my website, DrPaulaCPerez.com.

ADDITIONAL RESOURCES

If you would like more information on this topic, check out these resources:

Cloud, Henry and Townsend, John. *Boundaries in Dating: How Healthy Choices Grow Healthy Relationships* (Zondervan, 2000).

Harris, Kat. *Sexless in the City: A Sometimes Sassy, Sometimes Painful, Always Honest Look at Dating, Desire, and Sex* (Zondervan, 2021).

Hiestand, Gerald and Thomas, Jay. *Sex, Dating, and Relationships: A Fresh Approach* (Crossway, 2012).

Living Out. https://www.livingout.org/resources/articles/88/hey -single-christian-your-celibacy-is-uniquely- meaningful.

McDowell, Josh. *Why Wait? What You Need to Know about the Teen Sexuality Crisis.* (Thomas Nelson, April 30, 1994).

Treweek, Danielle Elizabeth. *The Meaning of Singleness.* (Downers Grove, IL: InterVarsity Press, 2023). www.ivpress.com.

Wiles, Jeremy. 15 Mind-Blowing Statistics About Pornography and the Church. https://conquerseries.com/15-mind-blowing- statistics-about-pornography-and-the-church

49-YEAR-OLD

Delayed Not Denied

DrPaulaCPerez.com

REFERENCES

Rosenbaum, J. E. (2009). "Patient Teenagers? A Comparison of the Sexual Behavior of Virginity Pledgers and Matched Nonpledgers." *Pediatrics*, 123(1), e110. https://doi.org/10.1542/peds.2008-0407

https://ifstudies.org/blog/does-sexual-history-affect-marital-happiness

https://ifstudies.org/blog/does-sexual-history-affect-marital-happiness

https://www.staugustine.com/story/lifestyle/2019/12/13/inside-purity-movement-and-its-effect-on-evangelical-women/2093750007/

November 01, 2020, by Kingdom Works Studios https://conquerseries.com/15-mind-blowing-statistics-about-pornography-and-the-church/

ABOUT THE AUTHOR

Dr. Paula is an educator, leader, speaker, writer, youth pastor, and pastor's wife committed to teaching, equipping, and challenging people to live life triumphantly.

She earned her doctorate in Educational Leadership, Management, and Policy from Seton Hall University. Currently she is an adjunct lecturer for the State University of New York at New Paltz.

In December 2010, Dr. Paula married her husband, instantly becoming stepmother to three young adults. Since 2015, she has served alongside her husband, Pastor J. Perez, at Faith Temple, a church in upstate New York. Dr. Paula took early retirement from her principalship to enter full-time ministry in 2018.

Dr. Paula and her husband are certified *Saving Your Marriage Before It Starts* coaches. Together they provide training for singles, as well as relationship support and coaching to couples.

To connect with Dr. Perez or to bring her in for conferences, workshops, retreats or other events, email info@drpaulacperez.com. Check out her website and social media links listed on her digital card: http://meetdrpaula.com.